Sing me a
Song of
Christmas

by Iain Whyte

Script by Janet de Vigne and Iain Whyte

First published in Great Britain
in 2000 by Parish Education Publications
Annie Small House
18 Inverleith Terrace
Edinburgh EH3 5NS

ISBN 0 8615 3301 1

Cover design by Heather Macpherson
Type-set by Christine Causer

Printed and bound in the UK by Scottish Studios

Sing me a Song of Christmas is dedicated to my mother Isa, and my father Wilson, who died in November 1999.

Their support and encouragement gave me the chance to discover music and make all this possible.

The Writer

Iain Whyte lives and works in Edinburgh with his wife Elaine, and his children Nicola and Louise. He regularly writes worship songs for use in his own parish church, where he performs with the praise band and is a member of the eldership ministry; his songs and musicals have also been taken up and staged with great success by local school groups. *Sing me a Song of Christmas* was originally written for use in the author's community. A trained teacher and former further education lecturer, outside of his musical commitments Iain is also the General Secretary of the Board of Parish Education of the Church of Scotland.

Acknowledgements

Personal thanks are due to:

Gill Cloke for her encouragement and efforts in putting the project together.

Brian Clark for all his help with the musical arrangements.

Janet de Vigne for her work on the script and editing.

Heather Macpherson for the design.

Christine Causer for setting the text.

SONG 1 Sing me a song of Christmas

All

Sing me a song of Christ-mas,__ sing of a vir - gin birth,

sing of a mi - ra-cle,__ of a God com-ing down to Earth.

Sing of a child in a man-ger,_____ and of ox - en stand-ing by, of

shep-herds and of kings, and of an - gels in the sky!

17 **Chorus**

How ma-ny flow-ers grow now on that bla-zing de-sert hill? How ma-ny seeds are

F Dm7 C C7 F Dm7 G C F

22

scat-tered on the wind? As we sing our songs of Christ-mas,__ can we hold our heads up

C F G C F C F Dm7

27

high? Or is what we say and do a sweet, ro-man-tic lie?

C F Dm7 C F D7 G

(Repeat ad. lib. instrumentally under dialogue.)

**Dialogue ends 'Narrator 3: ... as it was to the people
who lived through it all those years ago'.**

Turn quickly for Verses 2 & 3

Tell me an an-cient sto-ry,__ tell me of Beth-le-hem,_____
Speak of a child and a sav-iour,_ speak of a time to come, Of

C   F   C

High on a hill for all to see,__ yet__ sec-ret and un-seen.
peace, good-will to all the world, when the vic-to-ry is won.

F   C   F   D7   G   G7

Tell me of a sta-ble_____ where a my-ste-ry un-folds.
Speak to me in si-lence_____ as the world__ thun-ders on.

C   F   Dm7   C

13

Tell me of my his - to - ry, whose_ sto - ry lies un - told.
Speak and make me lis - - ten,_ lis - ten to your song.

F   C   F   G   C

17 **Chorus**

How ma - ny flow-ers grow now on that bla-zing de-sert hill? How ma-ny seeds are

F   Dm7   C   C7   F   Dm7   G   C   F

22

scat-tered on the wind? As we sing our songs of Christ-mas,_ can we hold our heads up

C   F   G   C   F   C   F   Dm7

27

high? Or is what we say and do a sweet, ro-man - tic lie?

C   F   Dm7   C   F   D7   G

(Slow down second time)

CUE: Narrator 3: ... the biggest thing to hit the planet since unleavened bread!

SONG 2 And he will be a king

And the an-gel said to Ma - ry,_____ Peace be with you, God has

blessed you._____ You will have a son, His name will

Moving on a little

be_____ Je - sus the Son of God._____ And

19
he will be a king, Like Da - vid was be - fore.
Am7 A7 D D7 G
27
Praise be to God, His king-dom will not end, This
Am7 D7 C G Am7 A7 D D7
35
son that God will send. He is the Lord.
G Am7 D7 C G

Picking up tempo, country-style rhythm

43 **All**

And the an-gel said to Ma - - ry,_____ Peace be with you, God has

G

49

blessed you._____ You will have a son, His name will

Am7   G

55

be _____ Je - sus the Son of God._____ And

G7   C   D7   G

he will be a king,_____ Like Da - vid was be -

Am7   A7   D   D7   G

-fore._____ Praise be to God,_____ His

Am7   D7   C   G

king - dom will not end,_____ This son that God will

Am7   A7   D   D7   G

send._____ He is the Lord._____

Am7   D7   C   G

CUE: **Mary**: I never dreamed I would ever be part of anything like this...

SONG 3 Might I ask you how you'd feel

Mary

1. Might I ask you how you'd feel, If an an - gel came to you And__ said you have been cho - sen by the Lord_____ To ful - fil a na - tion's dreams, A___ girl still in her teens! Who wants no - thing more than a - ny o - ther would?_____ Jo - seph was

all I thought I'd need, A fi-ner man you could-n't meet, Who would

C   Am

share my life and share my ups and downs._____ But then the

F7   Dm7   G

an - gel came to me, Told me all that was to be And in a

C   Am

mo - ment turned my des - ti - ny a - round._____

F   Dm7   G   C

33

Mine is not to won-der why__ I'll do what I must do_____ But

Dm / G / F / C G7

37

how can I ex - plain this thing,_ who will be-lieve it's true?_____ It

F / G / F / Am

41

sounds too much like fan-ta-sy___ for folk to un - der - stand._____ They'll

G / Am / C / F Dm7

45

say it's just a sto - ry,___ a game that I have planned. 3. But__

G / C / F G C / Dm / G7

though I am con-fused, I am rea-dy to be used To___

C   Am

serve my God as he would want me to._____ I'll take

F7   Dm7   G

up this hea-vy cross And__ pay the mas-sive cost And__

C   Am

praise the Lord my God for he is good!_____

F   Dm7   G   C

CUE: **Joseph**: Let's just go!

SONG 4 Bethlehem, city of Judah

1. Beth-le-hem, ci-ty of Ju-dah, the start-ing point of Da-vid's
ro-yal line, the an-ce-stral home of Jo-seph the joi-ner,
though he'd not been there for quite some time. No, he'd not been there for
quite some time.

(Keyboard repeats four times!)

Words and music © I. Whyte 2000

13

2. Jo-seph came with Ma-ry, his girl-friend, To fill in some forms he thought a

16

waste of time, But the bu-reau-crats from Eu-rope in-sis-ted That

19

eve-ry-one should sign up-on the dot-ted line, Yes, eve-ry-one should sign up-on the

22

dot-ted line. 3. With Ma-ry soon to have a ba-by, And

27

wea-ther that was ra-ther less than mild, They'd have to find a

30

place to stay, But Beth-le-hem was aw-ful bu-sy that day, Yes, Beth-le-hem was aw-ful

34

Mary & Joseph

bu-sy that day. 4. We knocked on doors of ho-tels and hou-ses, We

39

spoke to eve-ry-one that we could see. All we wan-ted was a room to sleep in, A

43

hos-tel, or an inn, or a B & B, A hos-tel, or an inn, or a B & B.

47

All

5. At last they came to a place on the out-skirts, A-way from the road in the

52

poor part of town. The inn was full, but they'd a room in the sta-ble Where at least they'd get their

56

2

heads down,___ Now at least they'd get their heads down.___

CUE: Narrator 3: There was no room for them at the inn.

SONG 5 Sweet little child of mine

(Joseph: Verse 3 only)

In a sta-ble in Beth-le-hem lies the King
Peace, good - will, Al-le-lu - ia!, He is born,

Mary

1. Sweet lit-tle child_ of mine, I can see me in your eyes.
2. Sweet lit-tle child_ of mine, you still have so far to go,
3. Sweet lit-tle child_ of mine, yet some-how not my child at all,

C   Am   C   G7

5

An - gels watch - ing ov-er Him and soft - - ly
God, our Lord, Em - ma-nu-el, the Cho - - sen

I can see all of the peo-ple I've been_____ I can see me in your
With all the ques-tions that dance in my mind, I won-der if you'll let me
Mine for a mo-ment and then you'll be gone,_____ Dash-ing my hopes on the

C   F   G   G7   C   G   G7   Dm

Words and melody © I. Whyte

Last time to
CODA 𝄋
8
sing:
One.
Mary & Joseph
eyes.
know...
wall.
What col-our is the wind?
What is the sound of
C
G
C
F
12
dark - ness? What col-our is the wind?
Where is the end of the sky? What
C
F
C
G
C
16
𝄋 CODA
(Start here)
wind?
What co-lour is the
col-our is the wind?
Sweet lit-tle child of mine.
(Repeat and fade)
F
C
Am
C
D. C. for V. 2/3

SONG 6 Shepherds' song

V1. Shepherds (can be spoken with a strong rap rhythm)
V2. Gabriel (spoken)

In the fields near Beth - le - hem, the shep-herds with their sheep,_____ Rest - ing un - der -
'Go you to the sta - ble there and seek the ho - ly child, For it is writ-ten

D   Bm   G   A7   D   F♯7   Bm

-neath the stars, they wake-n'd from their sleep,___ The an - gel of the Lord ap-pear'd and
he'll ap-pear, not great, but meek and mild.'___ They were a - fraid, but still they went, at

G   Bm   Em7   F♯7   Bm   A   D   F♯7

Gabriel (V. 1)

gave the dark-ness light._____ 'Peace be with you all, my friends, I bring glad news this
Ga - bri-el's com - mand And sought the child they'd heard to be the sa - viour of the

Bm   A   D   F♯7 Bm   A   D   Em7   F♯7

(V. 2 sung from here)

night.____ For born in Dav-id's town this day, and born of Dav-id's
land.____ They walked in si - lence to the inn, re - called the an - gel's

Bm   G   D   G

line,_____ the Sav-iour, Christ, the Son of God, now lies in Beth-le-hem.'
words,_____ They gazed in awe at what they saw and knew he was the Lord.

Al - le - lu - i - a! The an-gel voi-ces say. Al - le -
Al - le - lu - i - a! The an-gel voi-ces say. Al - le -
Al - le - lu - i - a! The an-gel voi-ces say. Al - le -

-lu - i - a! Christ is born to-day! Praise the Lord! Christ is born to-day!
-lu - i - a! Christ is born to-day! Praise the Lord! Christ is born to-day!
-lu - i - a! Christ is born to-day! Praise the Lord! Christ is born to-day!

CUE: **Melchior**: Oh, good grief...

SONG 7 The wise men

Wise Men

Far a-way to the east, Some wise men who'd been watch - ing

Saw a new star ap - proach - ing In the eve-ning sky.

So they gath-ered their friends, Said, 'We're going on a jour - ney,

Gon-na fol-low the star sign Where it leads us to...'

Where it led them to was Beth - le - hem And there it came to

rest, O - ver the place where Ma - ry lay, Her new-born ba - by

in the hay. So they ente-red the place, Saw the child in his

splen - dour And it filled them with won - der To see the son of

God. Then they fell to the floor And gave prai-ses to

heaven, For they were__ so cer - tain A-bout what they'd

seen._____ Cas-par, Mel-chi - or and Bal-tha - zar, The

wise men all knelt down And of-fered gifts to the new-born king Of

gold and fran-kin - cense and myrrh. As the mor-ning drew on,

A new day was be - gin - ning   A new hope he was bring - ing

Dm7   **G**

To a wait-ing world.   And the names of those men

C   **G**   **C**

Are re-mem-bered for e - ver   For the faith that they showed then

Dm7   **G**

rall.

And the gifts they bore...   Gold and fran - kin - cense   and myrrh!

C   **F** **C** **F** **G+**   **C**

CUE: **Messenger**: Yes, your Majesty... at once...

SONG 8 Herod was a jealous man

All / Messenger:

Herod:

1. He - rod was a jea - lous man, a - fraid of a - ny
2. This king would be born quite soon, near - by in Beth - le -
3. 'I'll have to act to save the day, I'll have to show who's
4. I'll send the word to all the land, so eve - ry - one might

threats,_____ He would-n't stop at a - ny - thing, what He - rod wants, he
-hem._____ How would it look if he stood by, what would folk think of
boss._____ To se - pa - rate in peo - ple's minds their pro - phets from my
hear,_____ That He - rod is no fool, he is a king who knows no

gets._____ Those wise men told him of a king, a child to take his
him?_____ A - no - ther king would sure - ly spell old He - rod's cer - tain
loss!_____ I need to take the up - per hand and crush this threat right
fear._____ Kill all the ba - by boys that you can find, and leave not

throne,_____ That he sim - ply won't al - low, this king must rule a - lone.
doom._____ A - no - ther king, a dread-ful thought, there sim - ply was no room!
now,_____ Like Mo - ses did those years a - go, I'll smash the sa - cred cow.
one_____ And do not show your face a - gain un - til the deed is done.'

Smash them, slash them, burn them, churn them, Tear them limb from limb,__
Wipe them from the pla - net, leave their mo - thers feel - ing grim.__

5. I

Verse 5

Da Capo (till Verse 5)

Herod hate to have to do this. It cau - ses me great pain. But

no poor i - mi - ta - tion will threa - ten me__ a - gain!__

Repeat Verses 3 & 4, then 'Smash them...'

CUE: **Joseph**: How can I cope with this? Our future is so uncertain...

SONG 9   Joseph's Song

Joseph

1. I see it writ-ten there on your face_____ I
2. I can-not un-der-stand these ___ things,_____ The

see it, but I can't read what it says._____
fears_ and the feel-ings that they bring._____

Can't you tell me, let me know? Just where will my fu - ture go?
What have I and Ma - ry done, To be blessed with you, my son,

Can't you see, I need to know?_____
God with us, the cho - sen one._____

Words and music © 2000 I. Whyte

Chorus

Lit-tle child, you know I'll love you, I will al - ways be proud of you,

G **A** **F#m** **Bm**

I will care for you as best I can,

Em **A7** **D** **D7**

I will put my arms a-round you, I will let my love sur-round you.

Em7 **A** **F#m** **Bm**

Lit-tle child, my own and God's own son.

Em **A7** **D** **A** **D**

3. Still, some-thing deep in - side me says,

The sun will clear a - way the haze

I'll live in faith and grasp the mo - ment, Love my God, my wife and son and

Pray that I can do what I must do.

Final chorus

Lit-tle child, you know I'll love you, I will al-ways be proud of you,

Em7   A7   D(7)   G(#7)

I will care for you as best I can,_____

Em7   A7   D   B7

Mary

I will put my arms a-round you, I will let my

I will put my arms a-round you, I will let my love sur-round you.

Em7   A7   D7   G7

love sur-round you, Mine and God's own son._____

Lit-tle child, my own and God's own son._____

Em7   A7   D   A7   A

CUE: Simeon: And sorrow, like a sharp sword, will break your own heart.

SONG 10 Here with us

All (Slow and reflective)

Ho - ly child of Beth - le-hem, a bless-ing for us all,_____ Son of God, Em -
Ho - ly child of Beth - le-hem, our pro - mi - ses ful - filled,_____ Hea - ven sent he
Ho - ly child of Beth - le-hem, we kneel be - fore your feet, A sym - bol of your

D   Bm   G   A7   D   F♯7   Bm   F♯m

-ma - nu - el, lies crad - led in a stall. In hum - ble - ness he comes to us, in
re - pre - sents all that our God has willed, We can - not grasp what this may mean, or
pre - sence here, where Earth and Glo - ry meet. Where shep-herds, kings and an - gels wings un -

G   Bm   D   F♯7   Bm   A   D   F♯7

weak - ness he is strong, He chal - len - ges our pre - ju - dice that we have held so
where this may all go We on - ly pray that we might stay and may - be come to
-ques - tion - ing look on Where pa - rents hold their new - born child and greet a spe - cial

Bm   A   D   F♯7 Bm   A   D   Em7   F♯7

Words and music © 2000 I. Whyte

long And ques-tions all our va - lues though he can't yet un - der - stand, That
know The sec - rets of his mis - sion here, the gifts that he may bring And
dawn. The world has changed in this one night, a new age has be - gun, The

Bm   G   D   G   D

he is sent by God to be the sa - viour of his land. God is
join with all the an - gel hosts in one great voice to sing.
Ho - ly child, Em - ma - nu - el, the cho - sen, God's own Son.

G   F#m   Em7   F#7   Bm   G   A

here with us, a light to guide our way God is

D   G   Em   A7   G   A

here with us, turn-ing night to day, praise the Lord God is here with us.

D   Bm   F#7   Bm   G   F#7   B

CUE: **Narrator 3**: ...wait for the next instalment of the story of Jesus - the Easter story...

SONG 11 Sing me a song of Christmas

Sing me a song of Christ-mas,__ sing of a vir - gin birth,

sing of a mi - ra-cle,__ of a God com-ing down to Earth.

Sing of a child in a man-ger,_____ and of ox - en stand-ing by, of

shep-herds and of kings, and of an - gels in the sky!

Page 31

17
Tell me an an - cient sto - ry, ___ tell me of Beth - le - hem,
C C
21
High on a hill for all to see, __ yet sec - ret and un - seen.
F C F D7 G G7
25
Tell me of a sta - ble ____ where a my - ste - ry un - folds.
C F Dm7 C
29
Tell me of my his - to - ry, whose _ sto - ry lies un - told.
F C F G C

33 **Chorus**

How ma-ny flow-ers grow now on that bla-zing de-sert hill? How ma-ny seeds are

F   Dm7   C   C7   F   Dm7   G   C   F

38

scat-tered on the wind? As we sing our songs of Christ-mas,___ can we hold our heads up

C   F   G   C   F   C   F   Dm7

43

high? Or is what we say and do a sweet, ro-man-tic lie?

C   F   Dm7   C   F   D7   G

48
Speak of a child and a sav-iour,__ speak of a time to come, Of
C C
52
peace, good - will to all the world,_ when the vic - to - ry is won.
F C F D7 G G7
56
Speak to me in si - lence___ as the world thun - ders on.
C F Dm7 C
60
Speak and make me lis - ten,__ lis - ten to your song.
F C F G C

Chorus

64

How ma-ny flow-ers grow now on that bla-zing de-sert hill? How ma-ny seeds are

F Dm7 C C7 F Dm7 G C F

69

scat - tered on the wind? As we sing our songs of Christ-mas,____ can we

C F G C F C

73

hold our heads up high? And re - call, just for a mo-ment, that the ba - by, the

F Dm7 C F Dm7 C F G

78

ba - by, the ba - by was born to die._____

F G F G C F C

Optional
Instrumental and vocal harmonies

SONG 1 Sing me a song of Christmas – TACET
SONG 2 And he will be a king

CUE: Narrator 3: ... *the biggest thing to hit the planet since unleavened bread!*

SONG 3 Might I ask you what you'd feel

CUE: Mary: *I never dreamed I would ever be part of anything like this...*

Sung to LA

Repeat from ✛

Add this one at the reprise:

(Verse 1)   (Verse 2)   (Chorus)
16   16   15

51

58

SONG 4 Bethlehem, city of Judah – TACET
SONG 5 Sweet little child of mine – TACET
SONG 6 Shepherds' song – TACET
SONG 7 The wise men

CUE: Melchior: *Oh, good grief...*

12

18   16

39

46   16

68

SONG 8   Herod was a jealous man

CUE: Messenger: *Yes, your Majesty... at once...*

SONG 9   Joseph's Song – TACET
SONG 10   Here with us

CUE: Simeon: *And sorrow, like a sharp sword, will break your own heart.*